# Verses From Kent

Edited by Angela Fairbrace

 Young**Writers**

First published in Great Britain in 2007 by:
Young Writers
Remus House
Coltsfoot Drive
Peterborough
PE2 9JX
Telephone: 01733 890066
Website: www.youngwriters.co.uk

SB ISBN 978-1 84602 952 3

# Foreword

Young Writers was established in 1991 and has been passionately devoted to the promotion of reading and writing in children and young adults ever since. The quest continues today. Young Writers remains as committed to the nurturing of poetic and literary talent as ever.

This year's Young Writers competition has proven as vibrant and dynamic as ever and we are delighted to present a showcase of the best poetry from across the UK and in some cases overseas. Each poem has been selected from a wealth of *Little Laureates* entries before ultimately being published in this, our sixteenth primary school poetry series.

Once again, we have been supremely impressed by the overall quality of the entries we have received. The imagination, energy and creativity which has gone into each young writer's entry made choosing the poems a challenging and often difficult but ultimately hugely rewarding task - the general high standard of the work submitted ensured this opportunity to bring their poetry to a larger appreciative audience.

We sincerely hope you are pleased with this final collection and that you will enjoy *Little Laureates Verses From Kent* for many years to come.

# Contents

| | |
|---|---|
| Kieren West  (9) | 80 |
| Katie Kay  (10) | 81 |
| Katie Humphreys  (10) | 82 |
| Jade Stratton  (10) | 83 |
| Priya Patel  (9) | 84 |
| Ben Slade  (8) | 85 |
| Kerry Anne Buttle  (10) | 86 |
| Kim Barnes  (10) | 87 |
| James Wendes | 88 |
| Danny Herbert | 89 |
| Megan Phillips  (9) | 90 |
| Monique Harris  (9) | 91 |

## Leesons Primary School

| | |
|---|---|
| Emily Mountney  (10) | 92 |
| Chloeanne Sherwood  (8) | 93 |
| Kearan Day  (9) | 94 |
| Geoffrey Watson  (10) | 95 |
| Matthew Hunt  (9) | 96 |
| Georgia Powell  (10) | 97 |
| Chloe Abbey  (8) | 98 |
| Jamie Aldridge  (8) | 99 |
| Harry O'Grady  (9) | 100 |
| Lewis Marfleet  (9) | 101 |
| Heather Godden  (9) | 102 |
| Emma Williams  (10) | 103 |

## Leigh Primary School

| | |
|---|---|
| Harry Colville  (10) | 104 |
| Thomas Coleman  (10) | 105 |
| Charlotte Doherty  (8) | 106 |
| Lydia Shacklock  (10) | 107 |
| Sasha Dane  (8) | 108 |
| Natalie Jobbins  (9) | 109 |

## Loose Junior School

| | |
|---|---|
| Kieran Watson  (7) | 110 |
| Charlotte Booth  (8) | 111 |
| Daniel Inglis | 112 |
| Ashleigh Burr | 113 |

## Lydden Primary School

| | |
|---|---:|
| Jack Smith  (9) | 114 |
| Lewis McLester  (7) | 115 |
| Becky Baker  (9) | 116 |
| Lauren Clifton  (9) | 117 |
| Samuel Huntley  (8) | 118 |

## Mundella Primary School

| | |
|---|---:|
| Billie Morland  (10) | 119 |
| John Benn  (10) | 120 |
| Jonathan Gotts  (10) | 121 |
| Qasim Ahmed  (9) | 122 |
| Harry Ransley  (10) | 123 |
| Ben Scully  (9) | 124 |
| Brandon Rye  (9) | 125 |
| Lucinda Barnes  (10) | 126 |
| Joshua Ames-Stewart  (9) | 127 |
| Chloe Reekie  (9) | 128 |
| Christopher Holley  (9) | 129 |
| Yasmin Miller  (10) | 130 |
| Mia Small  (10) | 131 |
| Luke Dix  (10) | 132 |
| Keiren Lewis  (9) | 133 |

## Old Bexley CE Primary School

| | |
|---|---:|
| Olivia Moran  (11) | 134 |
| Eloise Sibley  (10) | 135 |
| Louie Davis  (10) | 136 |
| Ellie Jones  (10) | 137 |
| Elyse Herbert  (10) | 138 |
| James Kennor  (10) | 139 |
| Michael Cann  (10) | 140 |
| Kevin Barnett  (10) | 141 |
| Samuel Richards  (11) | 142 |
| Zoe Hughes  (11) | 143 |
| Angus Dalgleish  (11) | 144 |
| Vanisha Patel  (11) | 145 |
| Jessica North  (11) | 146 |
| Georgina Brain  (10) | 147 |
| Elliot Beagley  (11) | 148 |
| Anthony Perry  (11) | 149 |

## Parkway Primary School

## Perry Hall Primary School

## West Kent Health Needs Education Service

# The Poems

# Horses In The Field

Horses like eating out in the sun,
walking round the field having some fun
they even like to have a long run.

A horse named Dolly is who I used to ride,
until one day she bucked and I fell off on my side,
I very much enjoyed riding Toby
I am now too big as he is a little Shetland pony.

I would like to own my own horse one day
to love it, groom it and feed it hay,
I did ask my parents but all they could say,
was wait until you're older because then you can pay!

**Danielle Smith  (7)**
**Holy Trinity Lamorbey CE Primary School**

# Snowy Days

I love to be out in the snow,
It makes my cheeks really glow!

Wrap up warm, so we don't get cold
To make a snowman big and bold.

**Annabel Power  (7)**
**Holy Trinity Lamorbey CE Primary School**

# Fun In The Snow

I love snow because it sparkles in the rain
and it's so pretty.
Snow is supreme,
snow is so good,
you have to wear a coat with a hood.
I love snowballs,
they are cool,
you need to wear warm clothes,
it is cold when the wind blows.

**Phoebe Daniels  (7)**
**Holy Trinity Lamorbey CE Primary School**

# Love

Love feels like a fluffy white cloud.
It sounds like a horse magically disappearing.
It tastes like marshmallow dipped in hot chocolate.
It reminds me of a family dinner with a burning, spitting fire.
It looks like a flashing sunset.
It tastes like a melted chocolate melting in your mouth.
Love is just magical.

**Hannah Butterworth  (9)**
**Holy Trinity Lamorbey CE Primary School**

# Sadness

Sadness is like a sun turning black forever,
It tastes like strong, mashed, horrible Brussels sprouts,
It looks like a melancholy funeral, tears rolling down everywhere.

It smells like black burnt toast,
It feels like cold metal striking on your scorching hand,
It sounds like a happy balloon bursting into thin air,
It reminds me of a deserted house.

Sadness can never be stopped.

**Laura Gladdish  (9)**
**Holy Trinity Lamorbey CE Primary School**

# Feelings

Sadness is like a burning candle,
Love is like buying your pet.
Happiness is like a laughing heart,
Fear is like a hot red spitting fire.
Anger is like a hard piece of black metal,
Hate is like *blood!*

**Alicia Clay (8)**
**Holy Trinity Lamorbey CE Primary School**

# Hate

Hate is like a stretching rubber band spreading around.
It feels like a freezing, hard metal spike.
It sounds like a moaning cat having its fur trimmed.
It reminds me of a piece of shattering glass.
It tastes like fiery peppers.
It smells like old mouldy food.

**Brandon Moocarme (9)**
**Holy Trinity Lamorbey CE Primary School**

# Love

Love is like a bird breaking free
It looks like snowflakes softly falling down
It smells like a creamy cup of cocoa
It sounds like the swooshing of the sea
It feels like a smooth pillow that's just come out of the wash
It tastes like a melted bar of chocolate
It reminds me of a happy child playing in the snow.

**Katie Moss (8)**
**Holy Trinity Lamorbey CE Primary School**

# Sadness

Sadness is like a stretching rubber band
It looks like a fly being eaten by a spider
It sounds like a person trying to learn the cello
It tastes like a drop of poison
It feels like a slug slithering around your hand
It reminds me of a tiger stalking for its prey.

**Ryan Dubbey (9)**
**Holy Trinity Lamorbey CE Primary School**

# Happiness

Happiness is like a fluffy white cloud sailing across a bright blue sky.
It looks like a bird breaking free.
It feels like a cosy blanket keeping you warm
                                    from a cold winter night.
It sounds like a kitten snoring while snuggled up with its family.
It smells like a cake that has just come out of the bakery.
It tastes like a creamy, luscious chocolate fountain
                                    dripping into your mouth.
It reminds me of a ship sailing across the deep blue ocean.
Happiness is just great.

**Ella Hall  (8)**
**Holy Trinity Lamorbey CE Primary School**

# Sadness

Sadness is like a chicken getting killed for food.
It sounds like someone scratching their fingers down a blackboard.
It tastes like light green mouldy Brussels sprouts.
It smells like burnt school dinners.
It reminds me of a dark, creepy punishment room.
It feels like a bed of sharp pins.

Sadness is a gloomy dream.

**Seif O'Reilly (9)**
**Holy Trinity Lamorbey CE Primary School**

# Anger

Anger is like a scorching desert in a howling sandstorm
It looks like a burning city with wild vicious flames
It tastes like hot chilli fizzling up in your mouth
It smells like a roaring volcano just about to explode
It sounds like a ferocious earthquake erupting fiercely
It feels like a brutal T-rex chasing you to death
It reminds me of someone being locked up in a dark, gloomy cellar
Anger is a virus that will never be stopped.

**Ella Coates  (9)**
Holy Trinity Lamorbey CE Primary School

# Love Is Like . . .

Love is a warm flowing river.
Love feels like a light fluffy cloud.
Love tastes like enjoying a frothy hot chocolate.
Love smells like lovely lavender and camomile.
Love sounds like birds singing in a tree.
Love reminds me of something beautiful.

**Lucy Lewis  (8)**
**Holy Trinity Lamorbey CE Primary School**

# Hate

Hate is like a black hole.
It tastes of Brussels sprouts.
Hate feels like a brick falling on you.
It reminds me of a blazing hot sun.
Hate smells of black smoke.
It has the sound of screaming
Hate, hate, hate.

**Chloe Burt  (9)**
**Holy Trinity Lamorbey CE Primary School**

# Sadness

Sadness looks like bright red
It feels like you're lost in a desert
Sadness feels like tears falling down my cheeks
Sadness reminds me of my brother hitting me
It smells like burning fire
Sadness sounds like someone crying white tears.

**Harry May  (8)**
**Holy Trinity Lamorbey CE Primary School**

# Hate

Hate is orange like a ring of fire
It comes and goes from a liar
It feels like the blazing sun and tastes like the number one
It feels hard and crinkly and smells like a fishing rod with a reel
And reminds me of a choir.

**Joshua Robertson  (8)**
**Holy Trinity Lamorbey CE Primary School**

# Sadness

It tastes like someone crying really loudly
It looks like a really rainy day
It reminds me of someone in a dark room
It feels like someone sulking
It smells like a burning fire.

**Peter Burch  (8)**
**Holy Trinity Lamorbey CE Primary School**

# Sadness

The colour of sadness is lilac,
Sadness reminds me of rain on holidays,
Sadness feels like snowflakes on your face,
Sadness tastes like strong onion burning in your mouth,
It looks like rain dropping on your window,
It sounds like a boy crying in the corner.

**Lauren Shelley (8)**
**Holy Trinity Lamorbey CE Primary School**

# Hate

Hate is a red-hot burning
It reminds me of a bright crash
It smells liko burning smoke
And tastes of red-hot chillies.
Hate feels like I'm on fire.

**Max Brian  (9)**
**Holy Trinity Lamorbey CE Primary School**

# Fear

Fear is like the colour of pure, clean white that never comes
                                    off you and sticks forever.
If you show your fear too much you're like a ghost, all empty.
It reminds me of two eager winds until one of them has won.
It sounds like shivering teeth.
It feels like a cold ice being outside all winter
And smells like you've not had a bath for two weeks.

**Rachel Cornwell  (8)**
**Holy Trinity Lamorbey CE Primary School**

# Cats

There was a little cat called Pippy
Who ran up the garden in a jiffy.
Ho caw a little mouse
Who ran to his house
And hid out of sight and stayed there till night.

**Harry Drummond  (7)**
**Holy Trinity Lamorbey CE Primary School**

# My Ship

My ship is
a medillion
that floats
across the sea.
My ship is a cheetah
running from its predator.
My ship is my pride and joy.
When you see my ship
ask me for a lift and see the world
in one whole day. When you get home
you will want to go again
when
you
find
you
have
no
more
money
to find out what the next stop is
and to find out the
capital of school.

**Brooke Brooker  (10)**
**Istead Rise Primary School**

# Animals

Animals, animals everywhere,
Animals, animals on the stairs,
Cats over here,
Dogs over there,
Animals, animals everywhere.

Cats and dogs running round the house,
Get on a chair, I saw a mouse,
Squirrels, foxes
Rabbits, birds,
Every kind of animal, we are lost for words.

Monkeys, monkeys jumping on the bed,
'Get down monkeys,' that's what Mum said,
Iguanas, snakes,
Lizards too,
Monkeys, monkeys, don't eat that shoe!

Tortoise, tabby and ginger cats,
Don't worry they won't ruin your mats,
Black, white, a mixture too
Don't worry they don't need a loo.

Budgie and parrot are types of bird,
Only parrots can say a word,
Woodpeckers and robins too,
Go away birds,
Shoo shoo.

**Hannah Clark  (9)**
**Istead Rise Primary School**

# The Sea Dragon

I am the dragon of the sea
I take down boats that I might see.

I leave my mark wherever I've been
The sailors I've seen were the worst of them all,
I took them down in one big bite
And off they went to their grave of might.

I tear the sails that I might meet
And the raging river meets the street,
They have a flood that wipes them off their feet
Floods their land and the sea rules the land.

**Luke Freere  (9)**
**Istead Rise Primary School**

# Devil

Scuttle from the house
He is scary.
He leaves squeaking noises
Where he goes.
He goes *hhhhhhhh*
Breathing fire
And he is freaky
I know.
He has prickles all over him
He goes *boom, boom*
He gets at the food
He goes *pshew*
On the ground
We always know
*Boosh bash*
*Bong.*

**William Hockey  (7)**
**Istead Rise Primary School**

# Funny Rabbit

Hopping, hopping, hopping
Munching through the grass.
Wiggle, wiggle, wiggle
Dancing in the grass.
Crunch, crunch, crunch
Gobbling, stuffing all the things
That I can.
Getting very fat
All I can eat.
Hop, hop, hop
I love to bounce
It's my favourite thing to do.

**Charlotte Barton  (7)**
**Istead Rise Primary School**

# Frogs Jumping Everywhere

Frogs are lumps
Lumps are frogs
Frogs jumping everywhere
Bound, leap
Dabble, paddle
Frogs are on the loose
Frogs, frogs
Slop, slosh
Sprinkle, shower
The frogs are on the lily pads.

**Archie Marshall  (8)**
**Istead Rise Primary School**

# The Devil's Adventure

*Tiptoe! Tiptoe!*
Goes the Devil
Taking all the jewellery
And all the expensive money.
*Smash! Crash!*
Goes the mirror
On the wall.
*Creep, crack*
There's someone there
Quick, hide!
The ghosts are awakening,
Flying away.
Gone!

**Sophie Fowler (8)**
**Istead Rise Primary School**

# Sneaky Royal Princess

The royal princess
Is as sneaky as can be
She doesn't frighten me
I can see she creeps alone
She tries to steal her family riches
She's sneaking up
To get the whole box.
Sneaky.

**Tamsyn Humphrey  (7)**
**Istead Rise Primary School**

# Silly Frog

Leaping
Jumping
Jumping
Everywhere
Jumping on the lane
And jumping in the air
When will I land?
I forgot!
I'm scared of heights!
*Splash, splash*
*Splosh, splosh*
*Plop!*

**Danielle Freere  (7)**
**Istead Rise Primary School**

# Robber In The House

Robber sneak
Robber balance
Robber coming in the house.
*Bang! Bang!*
Shhh, quiet
*Smash!* Oops!
*Wallop! Smash!*
Tiny footsteps
*Creak* the wood floor goes.
Sneak, quiet
Run, light
Hurry, quickly
Quick, shhh
*Bang! Bang!* the door goes.
Ouch!
Light.

**Cameron Stratton  (7)**
**Istead Rise Primary School**

# Sneaky Mermaid

Creeping
She is special
Swishing, hiding
Side to side
Tricking people
Splashing
Posh
Bubbling

Kind of beautiful
Sparkly.

**Paige Dore  (7)**
**Istead Rise Primary School**

# Diablo

Mum, I got one!
I got one!
I wonder how it works . . .
Spin, spin, weeee!
This is fun!
I wonder what else it can do . . .
Weeee!
Yay! I caught it!
Throw!
Fly
In the sky . . .
Down, down, down
Catch!
Whack, whack, across!
Look! I'm doing it!
I'm going to show Ben and George . . .
Wow! That's cool!
Now I'm going to have a challenge against
Someone else . . .
Spin!
Zoom, zoom
Throw . . .
Fly
In the sky . . .
Down, down, down
Catch!
Flick, flick
Whack, whack . . .
I win!
I'm the best!

**Lewis Shepherd  (8)**
**Istead Rise Primary School**

# Robbing

Sneak, sneak, tiptoe, tiptoe
Stealing all the sweets
*Rustle, rustle, snap, snap!*
Go the leaves and twigs.
Snatch, snatch, steal, steal
Uh-oh
Here come the cops!

**Marc Whitmore (7)**
**Istead Rise Primary School**

# Chicken Dinner

*Snap! Crackle!*
*Crack!*
Sizzling a chicken
*Bang! Thump!*
*Crash!*
Laying the table for dinner
*Wallop! Smash!*
*Rustle!*
Dishing up the dinner
*Yum! Delicious!*
*Tasty!*
Eating our chicken for dinner
*Bash! Smash!*
*Crash!*
Cleaning our dishes.

**Thomas Charlton  (8)**
**Istead Rise Primary School**

# Could This Be A Blizzard?

Could this be a blizzard
From the magic snow wizard?
If we don't go to school
I will feel like a fool.
It's up to the door
I think there will be a snowball war.
Could this be a blizzard
From the magic snow wizard?

**Isaac Ojo**
**Istead Rise Primary School**

# Wild Ponies

Wild ponies running through grass fields and trees
Wild ponies skipping and jumping, playing with the bees
Wild ponies sneaking round where all humans have been
Wild ponies gallop freely in places no one has seen
Wild ponies going everywhere on every free will they have
Wild ponies are all different shapes and sizes for you to see
Wild ponies stick together in groups of three
Wild ponies are not the same as you and me.

**Rhianne Newstead  (9)**
**Istead Rise Primary School**

# Butterflies

If you see a butterfly
in the pretty sky
flying so very high
wave goodbye.

If you see a butterfly
landing on a tree
you should quietly go and see
you might even see a bumblebee.

If you see a butterfly
fluttering all around
they may look small
but they won't hurt you at all
they just flutter round and round.

If you see a butterfly
fluttering round the house
do not get scared
because it's better than having a mouse.

If you see a butterfly
with beautiful small wings
they are prettier
than a couple of stupid old rings.
Beautiful butterflies.

If you see a butterfly
like a shiny sea
butterflies have lots of homes
with a front door and a key.

If you see a butterfly
as pretty as can be
look in my house
come look come see.

If you see a butterfly
as pretty as a fairy
their wings are just the same.
Do they all have a name?

I love butterflies.

**Alexandra Bullen  (10)**
**Istead Rise Primary School**

# Fairies

They're flying in the air somewhere
They leap, they jump, they spring
If you go over there you may hear them sing.

You can't see them on a pretty, pretty flower stem
Hide in a bush and just look for them.

They're always there so beware
So don't get scared, they have their own nest
So they are harmless.

Fairies are pretty but some may be a pity
They have small, little wings
But all you can do is sing,
Fairies are as pretty as a butterfly.
I love fairies.

**Gabriella Hicks**
**Istead Rise Primary School**

# Chatter Chatter Chatter

I'm a chatterbox
chattering all day,
I chatter at school
and in the hallway.

I chatter to my mum
and chatter to my dad,
he says, 'Why do you always
chatter chatter chatter?'

I chatter to my sis
I chatter to my bro,
I chatter to everyone
but they all say no!

I'm a chattering machine!

**Keeley Mason  (10)**
**Istead Rise Primary School**

# A Summer's Day

Once there was a summer's day
And the sun was brightly shining
Although the dawn had just broken
The bees were up there flying.

Once there was a summer's day
The flowers were growing fastly
By 12 o'clock it was red-hot
We even grew some parsley.

Once there was a summer's day
The trees grew big and bold
The beehives were full with honey
But the trees are going to mould.

Once there was a summer's day
It had nearly come to an end
The sun was going down too
I hope we have a sunny day again.

**Victoria Harrison  (9)**
**Istead Rise Primary School**

# The Teasing Reign

I had a friend at school who teased me a lot
He pulled my hair and called me names like Little Baby Tot
I tried to be his friend
And shared my sweets with him
But it never made any difference
Never, not at all
He would still go on teasing me
Until the end of school.

When I got home Mam asked me, 'What's wrong?'
I muttered, 'Nothing,' and kept smiling on.
I sat in my room and cuddled my toy
Then an idea hit me
On how to stop Troy.

I walked into class and pulled Troy's hair
He cried, 'Boo boo,'
And then came the big shock
I shouted at him, 'Hi Titchy Poo!'
I teased him all day until he finally gave in
And said, 'Sorry, I'll never tease you again,'
With a weary grin.

And now we have been friends ever since
And Troy hasn't teased me again
And even when I see a tiny glint of a tease
I shout, 'No more teasing!'
And give Troy an evil grin
He mutters, 'Sorry,' and keeps moving on
So that's how to stop the teasing reign going on.

**Madeline Pyke  (10)**
**Istead Rise Primary School**

# The Barking Dog

At night when I am fast asleep
I feel my body shake.
I hear a noise, don't know what it is
But it isn't a noise I make.

It roars and soars through my mind
It makes me go a little crazy.
I shake and shudder, feeling like rubber
Wanting to wriggle, feeling lazy.

I have these urges in my legs
They make me want to look.
I know I shouldn't, I know I couldn't
But I can't help wanting to look.

I looked, I looked
It's a wonderful sight.
I wondered what it was
What it's doing in the night.

It's a dog, it's a dog
It's a cute barking dog.
He's running wild round the garden
Jumping over logs.

**Jade Gard  (9)**
**Istead Rise Primary School**

# My Brother

My brother has a sword
My brother has a reward
My brother has a PSP
My brother has a Nintendo Wii
My brother has an England flag
My brother has an England bag
My brother has Heelies
My brother can do wheelies.

My brother has a teddy
My brother named it Freddy
My brother has a cat
My brother said it was fat
My brother has a dog
My brother thought it was a frog
My brother has a bed
My brother says it is blue and red.

My brother has a boat
My brother has a remote
My brother has boxing gloves
My brother loves doves
My brother has a car
My brother drives to the bar
My brother has a cat
My brother puts it on the mat.

**Marcus Thomas  (9)**
**Istead Rise Primary School**

# Class Clown

I'm a class clown
I'll cheer you up when you are down
I'll stand up in class
I'll sing a tune to shatter glass
I'll pull funny faces when it's boring
I'll keep you awake in class instead of snoring
I'll cheer you up when you are down
Because I'm your funny class clown.

I'm your class clown
I'll never make you frown
I'll never let you be sad
I'll always make you happy and glad
If I see a lonely person I'll be their friend
I'll cheer them up and promise I won't drive them round the bend
I'll never make you frown
Because I'm your really funny class clown.

I'm a class clown
I'll never let you down
And I'll cheer you up when you are down
You know who to look to whenever things go wrong
If you come to me I might sing a little song
So remember this poem whenever you are down
Always come to me, your funny class clown.

**Bethany Warren**
**Istead Rise Primary School**

# Schooldays

I wake up, wash my face
Put my bow just in place
Grab my bag, shoes and coat
Meet Cassie at the bus stop
While hearing Lassie the dog bark
The cop walking round
Waiting for Madman Sam.

Get to school, open my locker
Locker's a mess, oh God that's a shocker
Grab my text books, late for class
Oh well, time will pass
Get a detention, also shouted at
After school, grab a Big Mac.

Get once again shouted at
Tea's ready, cottage pie
A lousy day and now lousy meal,
So I sigh
I can only manage one mouthful
I call Cassie, gossip about people
Arrange a shopping trip, I'm very pleased.

Mum sends me to bed
I don't disobey what she has said
I decide to get an early night
So I lie down and turn off the light
I go to sleep, hopefully I've got that right.

**Chloe Walker  (9)**
**Istead Rise Primary School**

# Cat

My cat is funny
She tells me to tickle her tummy.
At night she lays on my bed
And lets me tickle her head.

She sometimes scratches
But she is still
My little pussycat.

I called my cat at meal times
She runs as fast as a rocket
Then she snuggles up to me
Almost inside my pocket!

**Evie Walsh**
**Istead Rise Primary School**

# The Midnight Sleep

As I go to bed
Fear pops in my head
As I go downstairs
I hear the creep of the chairs

Could it be a monster?
Could it be an alien?
Green, yellow, blue or red
Could it have eyes all over its head?

As I step onto the bare floor
I make my way to the door
I keep thinking, what could it be?
Or, is it meant to be up in a tree?

I slowly creep in
As I hear the rattle of the bin
I look inside, guess what I see?
It was the dog barking at a bee!

**Mia Canning**
**Istead Rise Primary School**

# Pokémon

I was swimming in the sea when I saw a Horsea.
I swam to shore, got my master ball,
Caught him and taught him all.
To the Pokémon centre we went
To heal Horsea, when well we sent
For Pikachu to come and play
For Horsea was captured and taken away.
I heard them making a sound
So I ran and jumped from the ground
Into the water to save my Horsea
He lived happily ever after with me!

**Lauren Wright**
**Istead Rise Primary School**

# The Big Bang

*Boom, bang, burst!*
The fireworks explode
On a Sunday night,
The baby is crying
And the dog has a fright.

My brother needs the toilet
My sister's getting hungry
My auntie's going mad
Because her hair's gone lumpy.

My dad keeps singing
This silly song,
You can tell that tonight
Is all going wrong.

My cousin Dill
Lost my nan's pill
I have a strop
With my uncle Dan.

And after all that
It ends with a *bang!*          ›

**Annie Banks  (8)**
**Istead Rise Primary School**

# The House

The house that I lived in,
Was creepy and old.
It was filled with cobwebs
With black and green mould.

The house that I lived in,
Was the scariest place.
It was filled with spiders
That I could go chase.

The house that I live in,
Is pink and sweet.
At half-past five
We sit and eat.

**Hollie Bettey  (9)**
**Istead Rise Primary School**

# The Good Poem

My mummy's an ancient Egyptian
Her insides are full of decay
When the weather is hot she smells such a lot
My friends won't come over to play.

My daddy's a cool Roman soldier
He loves his job so much
He fights, he's bright and he's pretty light
He's very strong and butch.

My sister's a cool school girl
Her name is Katie Good
Her teacher is mad, she is glad
That her teacher is pretty good.

**Jordan Rogers**
**Istead Rise Primary School**

# The Snow Snowy Day

Snow snow snowy day
I'm going out to play
And it's a snowy, windy day
Can I go out to play
With my friends in the snow?

I love the snow
It's fun to have snow, but not every day
The snow starts to fall down
It's still fun to play in the snow
Like sliding down the hill
But sometimes you get a chill.

**Daisy Haynes**
**Istead Rise Primary School**

# My Hopes Go Mad

I hope one day I will fly
Oh so very high
I want to touch the sky
Uh-oh, I hit the ground with a bash
I said, 'What a crash!'
So I get up and I see a shadow, 'What's that?'
Argh! It's a monster, so I run in the meadow,
'Oh no, a shadow!'

**Miles Keep**
**Istead Rise Primary School**

# Friends

Me and my friends always wear the latest trends
We meet up in the park but not when it's dark
We both go home and talk on the phone
Which makes our mums moan and groan
We both like to dance but we don't like to sing
At the end of the evening we both give our mums a ring
Then they come and take us home.

**Anisha Powar**
**Istead Rise Primary School**

# The Fairytale Town

Up, up, up in the sky
There is a fairytale town
Magic is beneath the air
You find fairies everywhere.

Up, up, up in the sky
Far away from below
Gold and silver in a chest
So much to count you can never rest.

Up, up, up in the sky
I never knew that fairies could fly
Their wings soar and swoop
So good they could fly through the hoop.

Up, up, up in the sky
Time for dinner
Time for bed
Goodnight my little ted.

**Olivia Berry (8)**
**Istead Rise Primary School**

# Anti-Bullying

Bullies are horrible so watch
And be careful because they hang about
Bullies are horrible, they kick and punch
Because they hurt you with a crunch.

Bullies are selfish, they never share
And they pull your hair
Bullies can be anyone
And they dare everyone.

Bullies pick on people younger than them
They call people names like a hen
And bullies think they're made of steel
But that's just not real.

**Henry Kelly  (8)**
**Istead Rise Primary School**

# Behind My Mirror

Behind my mirror
There is a magic world
Glitter and magic
And fairies curled.

Behind my mirror
All pink and white
I look in my mirror
Day and night.

Behind my mirror
A cool fairy came out
I told her to be quiet
But she tried to shout.

Behind my mirror
I'm getting annoyed
She's getting worse
She's throwing toys.

**Megan Lines (9)**
**Istead Rise Primary School**

# Funny Animals

I once saw a fat frog,
Sitting on a log,
I gave it a poke
And it started to choke!

I saw a small fly,
Up in the blue sky,
It was reading a book
About how to cook.

I saw a happy bird,
And everyone heard,
It was soft and fluffy
And very, very puffy!

I saw a slimy snail,
It was talking to a bug,
It got rather shy
And it started to cry!

**Bethany Bricher (8)**
**Istead Rise Primary School**

# Anti-Bullying

Bullies can hurt you, stop them before they do,
That's what you chould do,
Bullies only pick on people that they hate,
Tell someone before it's too late.
Bullies can make you feel scared
And they always get dared.
Bullies are selfish,
They kick and punch.
Bullies are mean,
They think they are keen,
They think they're made of steel
But that's not real.

**Lewis Shuttlewood (8)**
**Istead Rise Primary School**

# Don't Be A Bully

Don't be a bully
It's not very nice
So before you start you better think twice
I once was a bully
I liked to see kids cry
Just please don't ask me why
I didn't share, I didn't care
It just wasn't fair.

**Joshua Mayhew  (9)**
**Istead Rise Primary School**

# The Brown Mouse

He's as sly as a fox
Ho's as cheeky as a monkey
He lives in a box
And his name is Honky.

He's as brown as a brown bear
His butt is as curly as a poodle
He's as fat as a pear
And he likes to doodle.

He's got claws as sharp as an alligator's teeth
He's got whiskers as long as dogs' fur
All his friends called him Keith
And he hates the smell of myrrh.

He's got teeth as sharp as a knife
And he's looking for a new house
But he hasn't got a wife
Because he's a brown mouse!

**Amy Beswick  (9)**
**Istead Rise Primary School**

# Ballet Girl

I'm a little ballet girl
Sparkly
Kind
Beautiful
Silly
Funny
Love whooshing
In my dress
Sparkly ballet girl.

**Emma Weeks  (7)**
**Istead Rise Primary School**

# Dolphin

Wheely
Wavy
Diving, sliding in the water
Slimy
Sideways
Jumping, sliding in the water
Upwards
Eeee
Diving, sliding in the water
Sliding
Sneaky
Hiding, slimy in the water
Jumping
Hiding
Dolphin swims in the water
Twitching
Splashing
Dolphin playing in the water.

**Laura Skinmore  (8)**
**Istead Rise Primary School**

# Hallowe'en

It's Hallowe'en, it's Hallowe'en
The moon is big and bright
And we shall see what can't be seen
On any other night.

Skeletons, ghosts and ghouls,
Werewolves rising from their tombs,
Grinning goblins fighting duels
And witches on their magic brooms.

Maybe if you stay in bed,
Perhaps they will pass by,
Pull the covers over your head
And by morning away they will fly.

**Jake Shuttlewood  (11)**
**Istead Rise Primary School**

# The Hunt Of The Lioness

Sneaking slowly towards its prey,
On this African summer's day,
Then *bang!* like a gun, the race was on,
It kept on going as the sun shone on.

*Roar!* the lioness jumped on this beast,
And started to enjoy this victory feast,
Suddenly the big male lion came,
But then it just bounded off again.

So the lion just sat there enjoying her feast
Because she had caught a big wildebeest.

**Catherine Jack  (10)**
**Istead Rise Primary School**

# Night

Night gives me a mega fright
from the darkness that covers my house.
From the wind that will sway
and the mouse with its cheese
and the ghost that walks my passageway.

Why, the moon is all lit up
like a silver ball
and the stars all around it
are about to fall.

Snores from my mum
yawns from my dad
also dripping water from the kitchen tap.

As I look around my room
my eyes begin to close.

I have listened to all the noises at night
so now it's time for me to sleep tight.

**Jodie Nicholls-Young  (11)**
**Istead Rise Primary School**

# Metaphors In The Sky

The sun is a yellow ball
Light flying down the school hall,
The sun is a meteor
Coming down from space,
The sun is a Smartie
The yellow shining bright,
The sun is a daisy
Sleeping, being lazy.

The moon is a ball of cheese
Smiling, laughing at what he pleases,
The moon is a doorknob
A round twisting cylinder,
The moon is a massive rock
Craters here, there, everywhere,
The moon is a button
Two eyes staring at Saturn.

The stars are snowflakes
Settling on iced blue cake,
The stars are bubbles
Reaching so very high,
The stars are diamonds
Sparkle, twinkle, glitter,
The stars are sparks
Surrounding the fire at Mark's.

The sky is blue once again,
The world is turning,
The sky is plain.

**Emma Sewell  (11)**
**Istead Rise Primary School**

# India

I ndia rules,
N ights are lovely here,
D ays are always calm,
I ts country's food is really tasty,
A nyone would be welcome here.

**Benita Marwaha  (11)**
**Istead Rise Primary School**

# My Game

I'm the youngest
I've got to go first
I'm always hopeless
I'm cursed the worst.

Just like me
I'm stupid and lost
I land on tax
And pay the cost.

My turn's gone
The dice is there
The ship has sailed
To Leicester Square.

He had to buy it
My favourite land
He now holds the card
In his very hand.

The houses are laid
Same with the hotels
I've got to pass go!
'Money!' I yell.

I always dream
For precious Mayfair
But I've never won
I've never been there.

With a bolt and a flash
I lose all my fame
But who really cares
It's a Monopoly game.

**Sophie Winder**
**Istead Rise Primary School**

# The Big Bug Ball

The moon's shining clear and bright,
The music starts in the pitch-black night,
The bees are wearing all their best,
For the Big Bug Ball they are dressed!

The ladybirds flap their silk-red skirts,
Whilst caterpillars don some lucid green shirts,
The crickets play their violins
And the Big Bug Ball finally begins!

The hall is crowded, wings a-flutter,
The dance room floor is free of clutter,
Listen carefully enough, don't let your ears fall,
And you will hear the Big Bug Ball!

**Louisa Butlin (11)**
**Istead Rise Primary School**

# Who Are You?

Glistening all through the night,
I wonder what you are
Looking up, you seem so bright,
You are so very far.

First you look square, then you look round,
What shape are you supposed to be?
Staying so quiet, never making a sound,
Are you watching over me?

You move so fast in the velvet sky,
What colour can you be?
Please come back, don't go so high,
What colour, you didn't tell me.

I needed to know, so I looked in a book,
I now know what you are,
Twinkling and shining when I take a look,
I wish upon a star!

**Taylor Moore (11)**
Istead Rise Primary School

# The Football Match

Teams in the tunnel,
Hearing the crowd shout loud
While players came out of the tunnel,
Making the crowd proud.

The ball in the centre,
Players in place,
They wait for the ref to do his lace.

The game begins,
The team manager shouts out loud,
'I'm going to make a sub,'
While one person from the crowd
Gave up and went to the pub.

Red cards,
Yellow cards,
Coming from the ref's pocket,
While a girl plays with a Polly Pocket.

Half-time, the crowd has some wine,
John Terry goes for tea,
When he comes back on
He hurts his knee.

Lampard's in a hole,
Drogba runs into a pole,
While Fabregas scores 2 goals!

Arsenal 2, Chelsea 0.
10 minutes till full-time,
Lampard shoots but he's out of time,
Arsenal win the cup,
While Chelsea walk away,
And Arsenal shout, 'Hooray!'

**Jordan Thomas**
Istead Rise Primary School

# Owls About That

Tawny owl eyes round and bright,
Keeping lookout all through the night.
Moon and stars, the only light,
Take off in flight, just like a kite.

Barn owl, his head turning round,
Keeping lookout down at the ground,
Making sure others are safe and sound,
No enemies can be found.

**Jade Worswick  (9)**
**Istead Rise Primary School**

# School

School, I don't know where to start
Let's start with the school dinners
The peas are all mushy, the broccoli's all bushy
And if you think that's bad, listen to this,
The puddings are made of cardboard, yuck!

The teachers are pure evil
The head teacher doesn't know,
I tell my parents every night
But they say I have to go.

**Casey Willis (9)**
**Istead Rise Primary School**

# My Story

Well, it all started when I was swimming one day,
Hundreds of miles away from the bay.
Just swimming and playing, with my friend,
It was like the fun would never ever end.
But all of a sudden something appeared,
Something that I greatly feared.
I tried to scare them off by going bright red,
But it was no use, they caught me instead.
I was so scared, I fainted,
Grrr, they were the creatures I really hated.

When I woke up, I was in a place I'd never seen,
A place that I'd never ever been.
There were stranger fish around me,
But that's not the worst thing I could see
The strange creatures were staring at me,
That's probably the worst there could be.
I couldn't swim away, or even think,
But what I did, I made ink.
All the fish swam away,
But all the strange creatures did was sit and stay.
Then they started flashing things,
Small cuboid things.
The flashes dazzled me,
So I couldn't see.
And that's my story.
The story of Marina the octopus.

**Rebecca Saunders (10)**
**Istead Rise Primary School**

# Untitled

If they make standing still
An Olympic sport
I'll leave the rest still

If they make watching TV
Worth a gold cup
I'll win every year

If I'm made to run
In a competition
I won't move an inch

When I'm in the Hall of Fame
For being lazy
It will send me crazy.

**Samuel Hoyle  (10)**
**Istead Rise Primary School**

# The Monster

I once met a monster inside Asda,
I went up to him and said,
'Would you like to come over for dinner?
Make sure you bring your purple Mazda.'
So he came over and laid in my bed.
Goodbye Daddy,
Goodbye Mummy,
I'm writing this inside his tummy.

**Oliver Powell  (10)**
**Istead Rise Primary School**

# The Wiggle Sand Monster

One day I saw the Wiggle Sand Monster,
And offered it a pint of Fosters.
He threw it over his shoulder,
Onto a boulder,
Then ate the boulder instead.

The next day I saw him sucking a leech,
And when he saw me he ran to the beach,
Then he sprinkled some sand and started to wiggle
And after the wiggle he started to fiddle,
But I knew no more.

The next time I saw him, about February
He was swimming in the Red Sea.
He came over to me doing the backstroke
And gave me a poke,
Then he did the wiggle thing again.

We became friends and went to the bar,
Then everybody attacked him and he went, 'Argh!'
He fell to the ground and bumped his head,
Then I realised he was dead.
My loyal friend!

**Kieren West (9)**
**Istead Rise Primary School**

# Dog Gang

The dog gang strolls around,
Making sure there is no sound,
Barking, chasing all the cats,
Pushing, pulling all the mats.

In the dustbins all the time,
Other people get the crime,
Nicking food at tea and lunch,
What a horrible, horrible bunch.

**Katie Kay (10)**
**Istead Rise Primary School**

# Smugglers

If you see us spying,
On the cliffs for ships,
Don't you tell a lie,
Ask questions,
Answers flow by!

If you see barrels of wine,
Look the other way,
If you see bottles of beer
Don't you even stay,
If you see diamond rings
And crystal things,
We'll be back to play!

**Katie Humphreys  (10)**
**Istead Rise Primary School**

# Breeds Of Dog

Dalmatians love to run
Beagles are always playing
Chihuahuas are always howling
Staffordshire bull terriers are always flaming.

Labradors are loyal
Foxhounds at the hunt
Greyhounds at the race
Rottweilers always grunt.

Newfoundlands are large
Pekinese are too small
Basset hounds are short
Leonbergs are tall.

**Jade Stratton  (10)**
**Istead Rise Primary School**

# The Family Rap

My mum can rap this groovy beat,
When I listen to it I like to tap my feet.

My dad can hum this annoying tune,
When he does I'd rather be on the moon.

My older brother can sing this catchy song,
While my little baby brother goes ting tang tong.

So now I have to do my own rap
You know first I'd rather take a little nap.

**Priya Patel  (9)**
**Istead Rise Primary School**

# Fire

Fire burns
Fire hurts
Fire's dangerous
If you catch fire, stop, drop and roll
Don't breathe in smoke
Get down low.
Get out of the house
Forget your pet mouse
Call 999
You might get a burn
But you'll get out alive.
Don't take anything
Get it later
Call out the fire brigade
You won't regret it.

**Ben Slade (8)**
**Istead Rise Primary School**

# Untitled

My mum was kind,
My mum looked after me,
My mum was the best,
My mum made a nest,
My mum was put to rest,
My mum is always there,
My mum is up there somewhere.

**Kerry Anne Buttle  (10)**
**Istead Rise Primary School**

# My Life

*What I Look Like*

I have blonde hair with a little bit of brown,
my beauty deserves a crown.
I have a few freckles across my nose,
don't ask but I love to pose.
I have lovely blue eyes
and I don't eat pies.

*My Friends*

I have a friend called Honi,
she can be really funny.
And then there's Paige,
she can escape from a cage.
And finally, there's Hannah,
she is brighter than a banana.

*What I Like To Do*

I like to go out on my wheels,
but not after very big meals.
I love to sing all day long
and finish off with a loud bang.
I love to dance and groove all day,
I don't stop dancing until May.

**Kim Barnes (10)**
**Istead Rise Primary School**

# Anfield

Liverpool, Liverpool
My best player is Harry Kewell
We want to win
Because we want to have a big grin.

We don't like Chelsea or Man U
We just like Liverpool
We can't cheer you
Because we ant to have some fun.

Why do we love Anfield?
Because that is where we play
And why do we hate Stamford Bridge?
Because that is where Chelsea play.

**James Wendes**
**Istead Rise Primary School**

# School Dinners

Don't eat school dinners, just throw them aside
A lot of kids didn't
A lot of kids died
The mash made of iron
The peas made of steel
And if that doesn't kill you
The pudding will.

**Danny Herbert**
**Istead Rise Primary School**

# Winds Through The Olive Trees

Winds through the olive trees
Softly did blow,
Round little Bethlehem
Long, long ago.

**Megan Phillips  (9)**
Istead Rise Primary School

# Tears

Tears are
wet, not dry,
they're little
crystals from your
eye, they sparkle,
and simmer down
your cheeks.
I have tears when I'm
happy, I have tears when
I'm sad, I have tears when
I'm bullied by my mum or
dad, I have tears in my
bed. I have tears when I
get up, so I cry all the time.

**Monique Harris (9)**
**Istead Rise Primary School**

# Underwater - Haiku

Under the blue sea
angel fish swim gracefully
while dolphins follow.

Sea horses swim by
as the coral lies around
salty water flows.

Dancing and prancing
a dolphin lies with a rose
as bright as a ball.

Under the grey rocks
a starfish lies all day long
with its mum and dad.

**Emily Mountney (10)**
**Leesons Primary School**

# Yesterday

Yesterday I got blown up in a tree and nobody came to rescue me
Then I saw a cloud so I was very proud.
Then I saw a little girl, she was carrying a pretty pearl.
Then I saw a little boy, he was holding a funny toy.
Then I found out I was safe and sound in the cupboard.

**Chloeanne Sherwood   (8)**
**Leesons Primary School**

# Autumn - Haiku

Leaves fall down roughly
As autumn passes slowly
And it gets colder.

**Kearan Day  (9)**
**Leesons Primary School**

# Romans

R omans invade
O bey or be slain
M en at war
A lways built straight roads
N ever give up
S words and shields are ready.

**Geoffrey Watson  (10)**
**Leesons Primary School**

# Mustard

M ustard is nice
U nderrated, serve it on ham
S o very yellow
T hick as butter
A s wonderful as can be
R eally tasty with hot dogs
D elightful flavour I say.

**Matthew Hunt  (9)**
**Leesons Primary School**

# Leesons School

L earning is the thing we do
E verybody enjoys it
E very day we have some fun
S ocial events are number one
O bey the rules and be good
N ever give up on doing your best
S ucceed in school!

**Georgia Powell  (10)**
**Leesons Primary School**

# Things We Have Been Doing Lately

Things we have been doing lately . . .
Skipping in my garden
Playing on my trampoline
Biting my nails
Playing on my Heelies
Eating when I'm bored
Opening all my presents
Going to McDonald's.

**Chloe Abbey  (8)**
**Leesons Primary School**

# Things I Have Been Doing Lately

Staying up till 3am on New Year's Eve
Waking up my brother.
Helping my mum tidy up.
Doing bunny ears to my dad.
Staying up very late.
Going shopping with my mum.
Going on the Internet.
Laying in when I want to.
Staying up my friend's house.
Getting my Nintendo for Christmas.
Leaving the best till last.

**Jamie Aldridge (8)**
Leesons Primary School

# Autumn - Haiku

Autumn is chilly.
Leaves fall off the trees slowly.
While the wind blows hard.

**Harry O'Grady  (9)**
**Leesons Primary School**

# My Mother

M y mum is the best
O n the beach my mum had fun
T ogether we make cakes
H er hair is brown
E very day she listens to me read
R oses are her favourite flowers.

**Lewis Marfleet  (9)**
**Leesons Primary School**

# Heather

H ot at times,
E xcellent in every way,
A ppreciative for everything,
T iny but truthful,
H opeful to be a dentist,
E veryone loves her,
R eady for everything.

**Heather Godden  (9)**
**Leesons Primary School**

# Apples

A pples are round and crunchy
P icked fresh off the tree
P ips inside them are horrid
L ike little monsters they are
E verybody eats apples
S weet, red and green.

**Emma Williams  (10)**
**Leesons Primary School**

# Avalanche

Faster and faster the avalanche speeds.
Ice thrashes everywhere like bullets in all directions.
Great oak trees long lost.
Ice and snow hurtle through the valley.
Mountains consumed by snow with a mouth of ice.
Skiers try to escape,
Faster and faster the avalanche speeds.

**Harry Colville  (10)**
**Leigh Primary School**

# House Fire

The frantic flames scream
in the roaring fire.

The boil of the fire
munches everything in its path.

It crackles, it crashes
the fire rips up the carpet.

The fear of the people
rushes through their minds.

The house falls
the windows crackle and start to screech.

The red-hot flames sizzle
through the heated house.

It ripples through the landing
the paintwork peels off the walls.

The carpet burns into ash.

**Thomas Coleman (10)**
**Leigh Primary School**

# A Summer's Morning

The moon quickly walks away to the other side of the world.
Stars swiftly start to follow.
The sun awakens joyfully into the morning sky.
The clouds blush pink with happiness.
The birds merrily sing their lovely songs nearly all morning long.
Leaves gracefully dance in the gentle breeze.
The river slowly jogs down a hill.
Flowers whisper quietly to the grass, *it's summer,*
*it's summer, hooray!*
The cats peacefully start knitting with wool.
The dogs start playing a game of football.
The bees are humming because they don't know the words.
The wasps are happily eating apples.
The people start to awaken, it's silent,
For the people will never see a true summer's morning.

**Charlotte Doherty (8)**
**Leigh Primary School**

# Spring Day

Flowers are swaying gently in the misty breeze,
Breathing in the glorious spring day.
Water flowing, slowly down the stream,
While flowers whisper to the trees.
Baby lambs; take their first, timid steps on land,
While mothers watch carefully, counting each step.

Leaves leap and dance gracefully in the garden,
Twirling between the flower beds.
Trees sway their branches silently,
Rocking their babies to sleep.
The grass too is still snoozing,
Moving slowly and yawning yet still resting.

A rainbow sparkles and shines above us all,
Repainting itself over the world.
The winter fire cackles and pops,
Coughs, quivers then dies down.
Leaves gradually appear on the treetops,
Now the blossom is eager to show its face.

**Lydia Shacklock (10)**
**Leigh Primary School**

# Nature Is Alive

Flowers sway giddily in the mischievous breeze,
Pollen tickles my nose until I start to sneeze.

Flowers of every colour and perfume,
Snowdrops with their tiny white bonnets,
Daffodils twirl round in their fancy yellow dresses.

Tulips have their tea out of flowery pink glasses,
Wild sunflowers bow to the passing bees.

Daisies scamper across the lawn when giants come and tread,
Wild primroses dance in their beds and don't even turn their heads.

Reluctantly roses lay down petals, a bed of red for all to see,
Shy bluebells hide their faces in closed veils.

Orange blossoms, so sweet and pure stand stately on display,
To observe the children play.

**Sasha Dane  (8)**
**Leigh Primary School**

# Winter

The cold bites through the frosty surface
of the forest floor.
The pine-scattered ground shivers,
under a thick blanket of snow.
The elm trees groan as the wind
whistles around them . . .

Soft flakes of snow
scattered across the ground.
Some rest lightly on the bows of tall trees,
all dance as they fall . . .

The wind gradually becomes tired,
dying down here and there.
The snow eventually falls to a stop,
elm trees nodding off . . .

Long icicles hang
from the thick canopy of the forest,
silently melting,
shedding their tears,
for the coming of spring . . .

**Natalie Jobbins  (9)**
Leigh Primary School

# The Strange Creature

There's a person in a cottage,
With his feet in a kind of knottage!
He's got an intergalactic space controller
And it's faster than a giant roller.

All day and night it's *beep, beep, beep,*
Fingers on buttons, tapping feet.
I don't know what it's all about,
I wish I could go and try it out.

Can you guess who it is?
It's Uncle Robert!

**Kieran Watson  (7)**
**Loose Junior School**

# Mystery Man

Not so far from where I am,
There's a mysterious, strange man,
On Saturdays for breakfast,
He cooks his bacon in a pan.

He likes it all fatty,
And likes it in a bun,
His clothes are very tatty,
He has to wash them and be done.

He likes going on a motorbike,
But sometimes he is very scary (yikes!)
He likes eating mushy peas,
But he love love loves me!

So who is this creature,
Can you guess?
It's my dad!

**Charlotte Booth  (8)**
**Loose Junior School**

# Scary Creature

In a deadly and scary cage,
There lives a creature with a giant rage,
This creature has a menacing stare,
And when it walks it gives you a scare.

This creature has hair coming from every direction,
This creature is scared of its own reflection,
This creature chomps food down,
Then this creature gives a frown.

The only thing is it's my little guinea pig.

**Daniel Inglis**
**Loose Junior School**

# The Creature

Down a road there's a creepy shed
Where cobwebs hang above your head
There's spiders with an evil cry,
When you see them you'll be shy.

The creature has large feet,
The creature has his own seat,
He cannot hear very well,
He has his own bell.

The creature has lost one tooth,
He will knock you with a boof!
Well who is he?
*My grandad!*

**Ashleigh Burr**
**Loose Junior School**

# My Imaginary Friend

My friend Mister Snotty
He is very wacky.
He waits for me
When I go to school.
He waits for me
When I come back from school.
He belches his ABC.
He knows it very well
Oh yes indeed
He knows it very well.

**Jack Smith  (9)**
**Lydden Primary School**

# Dinosaur Dreams

Once I had a dream about a dinosaur,
He was very weird, he was very lazy.
He had a neck about as tall as me!
He even slept in my bedroom.
He loved me so much.
He often ate breakfast with me.
He was so weird he made my head fall off!

**Lewis McLester (7)**
**Lydden Primary School**

# The Weird Day

My mum moaned and made my moody mice mutter.
Peg the leg plodded and pleaded while Penny poked Percy.
Ned the noddy nobody nattered and clattered.
Debby the dog demanded dunking doughnuts.
Curtis the cow coughed and called the other cows.
Sidney the snake slithered slowly sideways.
Pebble the penguin pecked Peter's pies.
Kim the king kicked Kevin.
Gerry the gerbil gnawed gleefully.
Danny the dinosaur dug ditches.
Ron the rabbit raced to the rum.
Charley the chinchilla crunched the cage.
Natasha the nice nobbly narwhal nattered noisily.
Vicky the vole captured caterpillars.
Hazel the happy horse hopped happily.
Sally the selfish sea horse swam sideways.
Danielle the dogfish danced delightfully.

**Becky Baker (9)**
**Lydden Primary School**

# My Wacky World

In my wacky world, this is how it goes
Here it is, this is what to show
In the streets there are weird things
There are things that go clang, and things that go ping

There's a talking, walking book,
He really likes to cook,
He also likes to toddle
On the catwalk and be a model
He loves to scream and shout
Open up his covers and let it all out!

There's also a flying bunny
Who is very funny
He likes to chat and play
Every single day
He likes to fly up high
So far up he needs an air supply

There is a walking whale
He would win a race, never fail!
He really likes to walk
He always seems to talk
He'd like to run a mile
But he'll go so fast he'd end up in a stile

There is a friendly fairy, but she likes to swim
She'd go over water, or rather she would skim
She hates to fly up high
But we really don't know why?
She can swim very fast
You would not know she'd gone past
That's my wacky world right up in my mind
If you tried to find it you better be kind.

**Lauren Clifton  (9)**
**Lydden Primary School**

# World

The world is a wonderful thing
We walk on it and God made it.
It is big and round
Without the world
You and me would not exist.
On the world people walk,
Drive,
Play,
Learn,
Love
And live on it,
But just remember
The world is a wonderful thing!

**Samuel Huntley (8)**
**Lydden Primary School**

## Passion

Passion is like fire exploding from a volcano.
Passion sounds like waves splashing against a wall.
Passion smells like sweet strawberries in the morning.
Passion looks like a purple sunset calming the evening sky.
Passion feels like freedom.
Passion reminds me of my nan who I love.

**Billie Morland  (10)**
**Mundella Primary School**

# Sadness

Sadness is like the night-time sky
Sadness smells like boiled eggs
Sadness sounds like a noisy TV
Sadness tastes like poison
Sadness looks like darkness
Sadness feels like someone being hurt
Sadness reminds me of when I cut myself.

**John Benn (10)**
**Mundella Primary School**

# Darkness

Darkness is red like blood.
The sound, like thunder crashing on rocks.
The taste is bitter, sour and rotten eggs.
It smells like rotten fruit and mouldy beans.
It looks like rotting grass.
It feels like squelchy goo.
It reminds me of a dead slug.

**Jonathan Gotts  (10)**
**Mundella Primary School**

# Darkness

Darkness is red like garbage.
It tastes like fish.
It smells like a dead bird.
It looks like a shadow.
It feels like someone behind you.
It reminds me of a boy getting hit.

**Qasim Ahmed  (9)**
**Mundella Primary School**

## Anger

It sounds like loud music banging the walls.
It tastes like cockroaches in your teeth.
It smells like sour milk.
It looks like a hairy black spider.

**Harry Ransley  (10)**
**Mundella Primary School**

# Craziness

Craziness is green like a colouring pen.
Craziness sounds like happiness.
Craziness tastes like sour sugar.
Craziness smells like chicken.
Craziness looks like you're on fire.
Craziness feels like hot water.
It reminds me of happiness.

**Ben Scully (9)**
**Mundella Primary School**

# Fun

Fun is a red-hot sun,
It sounds like rock music,
It tastes like a lovely burger,
It smells like freshly cut grass,
It looks like a merry-go-round,
It feels like a red-hot sun,
It reminds me of a big beautiful light.

**Brandon Rye  (9)**
**Mundella Primary School**

# Fun

Fun is yellow like the sun,
It sounds like little children playing football,
It tastes like an ice cream sundae,
It smells like a hot summer's day,
It looks like fairies playing in the garden,
It feels like a dream in your sleep,
It reminds me of a holiday in London.

**Lucinda Barnes  (10)**
**Mundella Primary School**

# Fear

Fear is brown like a gorilla.
It sounds like an alarm clock going off.
It smells like a foot.
It tastes like a slug.
It looks like black.
It feels like eating blood.
It reminds me of a monster eating me.

**Joshua Ames-Stewart  (9)**
**Mundella Primary School**

# Fear

Fear is grey like a nightmare lasting for hours,
It tastes like a rotten apple,
It smells like puke that's been left for 1000 years,
It looks like a black hole coming to swallow me up,
It feels like a glass bottle being smashed over my head,
It reminds me of a haunted house playing a piano.

**Chloe Reekie  (9)**
**Mundella Primary School**

# Anger

Anger is red like blood,
Anger tastes like organs being mashed up,
Anger feels like a spear point with bones as charms,
Anger smells like Jerkey's revenge,
Anger sounds like someone heartbroken,
Anger looks like a guy being murdered
And worst part of this poem is . . .
Anger reminds me of aliens killing innocent people
And *I'm next!*

**Christopher Holley  (9)**
**Mundella Primary School**

# Happiness

Happiness is bright, multicoloured and full of joy and laughter.
Happiness sounds like party music vibrating through the walls.
Happiness tastes like bagels and crisps and party food.
Happiness smells like fresh perfume running through the air.
Happiness looks like light fluffy clouds floating through the sky.
Happiness feels like fairies are always by your side.
Happiness reminds me of being safe with friends around you.

**Yasmin Miller (10)**
**Mundella Primary School**

# Anger

Anger is red like blood.
It sounds like banging.
It tastes like revolting snails.
It smells like dusty castles.
It looks like a haunted mansion.
It feels like touching a huge furry spider.
It reminds me of being lost in a big forest.

**Mia Small (10)**
**Mundella Primary School**

# Darkness

Darkness is black like shadows.
Darkness is like someone shouting.
Darkness tastes like slimy goo.
Darkness smells like mouldy egg and milk.
Darkness looks like a big creepy shadow.
Darkness feels like a horrible black blur.
Darkness reminds me of someone dying in their bed
                              at night when nobody knows.

**Luke Dix  (10)**
**Mundella Primary School**

# Fun

Fun is light colours, like fish.
It sounds like someone laughing.
It tastes like broccoli.
It smells like someone dancing.
It feels like someone playing with me.
It reminds me of when I was playing football
and when I was good.

**Keiren Lewis  (9)**
**Mundella Primary School**

# My Cat

My cat really loves cod fish.
She eats it from her pink dish.
My cat's name is Tallulah.
She loves my bendy ruler.

My cat is one-year-old.
At night she gets quite cold.
I love my cat very much.
She is fluffy to touch.

She is sweet, she is cute.
She loves to play with fruit.
I lover her miaow, I love her purr,
I love all of her.

**Olivia Moran  (11)**
**Old Bexley CE Primary School**

# Fairies

Fairies flying through the air.
All of them with different hair.
Some with blonde wavy locks.
Some are mad in the shape of a box!

Fairies are pretty enough
But are they tough enough?
Some with very powerful jewels.
Other's jewels are just plain fools.

Fairies wave their magic wands
And make unusual things come.
And they say the magic words.
Now here comes some talking birds!

Fairies can fly so high in the sky
But I really can't fly that high.
I want to be a fairy.
I could make my dad's back hairy!

But if I were a pretty fairy
I wouldn't be any more darey.
I wouldn't go to tea with friends
My magic would drive them round the bend.

I'm happy the way I am.
Going for days out and eating my favourite ham.
Picnics, laughing and going to the park
And listening happily to my dog bark.

But I still love fairies.

**Eloise Sibley (10)**
**Old Bexley CE Primary School**

# Clowns

I've seen clowns before
They're bound to make you laugh
You've really got to see them
They'll make your dog bark.

I laugh a lot at the circus
Especially at the clowns
They really are funny
They never ever frown.

I've been to the circus
The clowns are always there
They're the most important part of it
You'll laugh, it's never rare.

Clowns are the best!

**Louie Davis  (10)**
**Old Bexley CE Primary School**

# Truffle The Hamster

T ruffle is my hamster!

n unning makes Truffle tired.

U nhealthy hamsters are more likely to die.

F leas can be awful for your hamster but mine does not have fleas.

F or Truffle we change his water every other day.

L ittle hamsters are cute!

E ating food is Truffle's hobby.

J ones is Truffle's last name.

O nly one Truffle Jones!

N ormal hamsters live for two years.

E veryone should have a hamster for experience.

S ome people think Truffle is scary.

**Ellie Jones (10)**
**Old Bexley CE Primary School**

# Granny

Every day I hold my breath
I wait for the minute
When in comes *Granny!*

Even though she's very deaf
She will always scare me
Then in comes *Granny!*

Teatime is when every day
It is time for her to say
Come here and give me a kiss
Granny, I'd rather give it a miss!
She only does it to torture me
My excuses are I need a wee!
But she still sits there in her chair
She's waiting to kiss me everywhere
I'll never get away from her
In her head will it never occur -
That her kisses are yuck
They taste like slimy muck
I wish that she didn't come
Or she just kissed my mum
I always rush upstairs
When in comes *Granny!*

**Elyse Herbert (10)**
**Old Bexley CE Primary School**

# My Little Hamster

My hamster's name is Treat,
He's really, really sweet,
My hamster is light brown,
He never has a frown,
I comb his hair up neat.

I clean out his cage,
While he runs around with rage
In his little ball,
Although he isn't very tall,
I play with him for age . . .

                                        . . .s.

**James Kennor  (10)**
Old Bexley CE Primary School

# My Cat

I have a cat
his name is Pat
he clawed my rug
broke my mug
and he sat
on the mat
looking at me
very guilty
you're my foe
I let him go
I heard a crash
went like a flash
opened the door
almost swore
kicked him out
and had a shout.

**Michael Cann  (10)**
**Old Bexley CE Primary School**

# A Dog Called Lucky

There was a dog called Lucky
He met a dog called Tucky
Then wanted to play hockey
And then got Tockey
On the way back they both were mucky.

Lucky went on a day trip
Then he got sick
But did it as a trick
Everyone ran and screamed
Then he peaked.

**Kevin Barnett  (10)**
**Old Bexley CE Primary School**

# 5 Things Not To Do In A Test

5 things not to do in a test.

1 Try not to stick your paper down your vest.
2 Or to copy someone 'cause they're the best,
3 And don't make your test into a plane,
  Because you will get the blame,
4 So you're on question 2,
  Don't pretend that you've got the flu.
5 And don't write a message to your pal,
  Stop looking at Mr Capal.

Just take it in your stride,
Then you will feel the pride,

Because then you will feel
Without the help from Mrs Maceel

That you've . . . done it!

**Samuel Richards  (11)**
**Old Bexley CE Primary School**

# The Soppy Film

I saw a film,
It was hilarious,
My friends could hardly understand it,
But neither could I!

Then my friends started to throw popcorn,
Oh no!
The people behind started to get fed up,
But we didn't care.

It got soppy at the end,
My friend pretended to cry,
We knew it hadn't finished because
The fat lady hadn't sung!

'Don't forget your own back.'
'Who was throwing popcorn at me?'
'Oh no . . .'

**Zoe Hughes  (11)**
**Old Bexley CE Primary School**

# The Grand Old Duke Of Kent

The grand old Duke of Kent
He stuck his feet in cement
He jumped himself to the top of the hill
He rolled back down again.
When he jumped up he was there
When he rolled down he was bare
When he was only halfway up he was in his pink underwear.

**Angus Dalgleish (11)**
Old Bexley CE Primary School

# Diamonds

Diamonds, they sparkle and shine,
So popular you'd do a crime,
Just to have a priceless gem,
Perfect gift for a good friend.

Diamonds come in all colours and shapes,
Red, pink, purple, even grape!
Spheres, cuboids, cylinders, perfect shapes for a ring,
A girl's gotta have her favourite thing!

**Vanisha Patel  (11)**
**Old Bexley CE Primary School**

# My Dog

My dog is white with brown patches,
The stick I throw which he catches,
His eyes glisten as he sees me,
Stroking him completely.

His ears prick when the door goes,
His tail swerves in a nice pose,
The fur ruffles along my hand,
Running on the open land.

**Jessica North (11)**
**Old Bexley CE Primary School**

# My Funny Family

My mum and dad
always write things in a pad
they sometimes give me what I like
but never a new bike.

The reason that I never bite
is because I just hate to fight
so one day when the washing's out
I'll turn my brother inside out.

That way he can see why I get upset
then look it up on the Internet
and won't be able to fight anymore
so I'll bang his head against the door.

**Georgina Brain  (10)**
**Old Bexley CE Primary School**

# Two Frogs

There was a young frog from Kent,
Who thought that Lent was Advent!
He said, 'Happy Christmas'
'Twas eaten by Bagpuss
And into his tummy he went!

There once was a frog called Frankie,
Who just loved a good cup of tea!
He gulped down a cuppa,
Then went for his supper,
Then went for a swim in the sea!

**Elliot Beagley (11)**
Old Bexley CE Primary School

# My Trip To Florida

F lorida has tho best roller coasters.
L ots of people have suntans.
O rlando is a place in Florida.
R oads are a lot wider there.
I love Florida.
D riving age is 16 years old.
A eroplane is how I got there.

S hikra is a roller coaster in Florida.
H ulk is another scary ride.
I t is 205ft high.
K ids love them.
R eally scary.
A ll of the roller coasters are high.

**Anthony Perry  (11)**
**Old Bexley CE Primary School**

# I Want A Pet

'Mummy, Daddy I want a pet.'
'Dear, think about poor Julliet
The fish that lived for just a day
When you brought her out to play.'

'Grandpa, Granny I want a pet.'
'Love, think about dear Marriet
The dog you lost when at the park
When you went there after dark.'

'Auntie, Uncle, I want a pet.'
'Dear, think about young Lilliet
The mouse you took into the garden
When you went to make a den.'

'Nanny, Grandad, I want a pet.'
'Love, think about small Perriet
The cat you hit around the head
When you went upstairs to bed.'

'Okay dear, you can have a pet.'
The next day we went to the vet
My mum bought me a potted plant.
'You must look after it,' said my aunt.

I tried to look after it, I really did
But after all I am a kid.
I went downtown to buy some bread
But when I returned the plant was dead!

**Lizzy Howard  (11)**
**Old Bexley CE Primary School**

# The Tay Bridge

A train was crossing Tay Bridge in 1879
That day will be remembered for a very long time.
The wind was blowing
The supports were going,
And down it went,
All broken and bent.

The people who live near the Tay,
Showed a great deal of dismay.
'Strong bridges we must build,
To stop people being killed.
I cannot bear to see
Dead bodies so close to me.'

Although this was an accident,
I hope lessons were learnt,
About how to build bridges strong,
So no more break, or go wrong.

**Alexander Castallack-Ridgley  (11)**
Old Bexley CE Primary School

# My Pirate

I once met a pirate,
Who sailed the seven seas,
He had a big bushy beard,
And was rather fond of bees.
And this very pirate,
Who sailed the seven seas,
Was looking for treasure,
And was called Captain McKnees!

The treasure he said,
Was deep, deep underground,
It was worth a fortune,
But it has never been found!
He had a big large map,
With 'X' marking the spot.
I thought I knew the island,
So I said, 'I know that dot!'

'Nah!' said Captain McKnees,
'How'd you know things like that?
You're not even a pirate,
McBat didn't know. Hmmm! Bat!'
'I'm telling you!' said I.
'It's in my pirate book!'
'You think you know more than me?'
'I've got the book, take a look!'

'By golly you are right!'
'See, didn't I just say!
I was right after all!
So I'll give you the book! Hey!
What are honest friends for?
But I hope this helps you,
Find your great, precious treasure,
But I must go, toodooloo!'

'Wake up! Wake up!' says Mum,
Now I realise it's a dream.
Hope you've learnt a few lessons
One is, even though some things seem supreme,
They might really have sense!
Friends should always stick together.
No matter what happens in the future.
Now you've heard my story that will remain forever!

**Zeinab Ruhomauly  (10)**
Old Bexley CE Primary School

# Darkness

Darkness is dull,
Darkness is black,
Darkness is not very tasty,
Darkness tastes of sad people,
Darkness reminds me of the dull time that I had,
Darkness smells like tears,
Darkness also reminds me of sad times.

**Callum Putney  (11)**
**Old Bexley CE Primary School**

# Andrew

The laughing clown,
The happy bear,
The unknown figure that gives you a scare!
Like a chatty monkey that just won't stop,
A smelly gas that goes *pop!*
Those are the funny things my brother does.

But this is what he's like when he doesn't have his buzz,
Remote snatching,
Chocolate eating,
Sarcastic jokes,
Hurtful pokes,
Guitar twanging,
Always nagging . . . *Andrew!*

**Emma Hickey (11)**
**Old Bexley CE Primary School**

# Funfairs

Toffee apples on a stick,
Lollipops that you can lick.

Ice cream melting on my tongue,
Greasy burgers in a bun.

Crispy apple pies and custard,
Hot dogs are covered in mustard.

Candyfloss whirls round and round,
Litter's dropping on the ground.

Popcorn's popping in a pan,
Coca-Cola in a can.

Bubblegum and cherry powder,
People's voices getting louder.

Fritters, waffles, chewing gum,
This is what I call fun.

**Caitlin Wilcock (11)**
**Old Bexley CE Primary School**

# Happiness

Happiness is yellow like the shining sun,
Happiness looks like fun and smiles,
Happiness tastes like iced buns,
Happiness feels like flattery and a whole bowl of love,
Happiness smells like flowers, as bright and colourful as rainbows,
Happiness sounds like laughter, as cheerful as can be.
Happiness reminds me of fun and laughter,
Bright as the sun, as long as the Earth.

**Calum Wallace  (10)**
**Old Bexley CE Primary School**

# The Darkness

Darkness is dark like the impending shadow
chasing you, minute by minute.
Darkness reminds me of a night-time roller coaster
slowly bringing you closer to tragedy.
Darkness tastes like the times in your life when you are down.
Darkness looks like a horrid person
following you everywhere you go, slowly trapping you in.
Darkness smells like depression and there is no way through.
Darkness sounds like a train on a train track,
screeching as it slows down.

**Harry Chapman  (11)**
**Old Bexley CE Primary School**

# Darkness Of The Sea

Darkness is black like a sea of surrounding doom,
A force of increasing peril that will fill an empty room.
Darkness fills the world with dread and suddenly woe is me,
With the sound of horseback and the darkness of the sea.
In a land of shadows and a mess of gothic walls,
Dark is like a sand timer as each small grain will fall.
Darkness has a smell that will drive someone insane,
Hear the deadly sound as the waves come around again.
See the haunted faces of the people in the streets,
Was it the waves of darkness you emotionally meet?

**Alex Kemsley  (11)**
**Old Bexley CE Primary School**

,

# Pet Shop

*(Inspired by 'Jabberwocky' by Lewis Carroll)*

'Twas noisy and the cats and dogs
Did miaow and bark in the cages
All timid were the mice and rats
And the colourful birds a-squawking.

Beware the fearsome pup my son
The tongue that licks, the tail that wags
Beware the pussycat and friends
The furious animal.

He took his wad of cash in hand
Long time he took to choose his breed
So rested he on a nearby chair
And sat awhile in thought.

And as in uffish thought he sat
The frightening pup with pointed ears
Came rushing across the pet shop floor
And barked as he came.

Calm down, calm down
And do not jump
The playful pup went *woof, woof, woof*
He picked it up and stroked his head.

And has thy chosen the dog he wants
O come to my arms my youngest pup
O fabulous day, hip hip hooray
He chortled in his joy.

**Jessie Seales  (11)**
**Old Bexley CE Primary School**

# The Riddle Of Doom

The more you take out the bigger it gets
Deeper and deeper it gets, blacker and blacker
Then you hit something hard.
The thing is sharp, it feels hairy.
The thing has gone
There are piles around it
It's really big now, massive
Growing every second
Bigger and bigger
Getting closer and closer
It's very scary
What is it? What is it?
Just what is it?

**Thomas Ousby (11)**
**Old Bexley CE Primary School**

# Feelings

Love is red like a rose.
Love feels like a burning sensation for your one and only love.
Love reminds you of all the exhilarating times you've had in your life.
Love looks like two people who are having the time
of their life together.
Love smells like a miracle with two people who are in love
with each other.
Love tastes like melted chocolate with strawberries as well.
Love sounds like fireworks bursting everywhere.
Fun is yellow, like a child's bright face,
Fun sounds like children screaming and chatting all day long.
Fun tastes like Angel Delight with sprinkles all over it.
Fun and love makes everybody *happy!*

**Lauren Smith (11)**
**Old Bexley CE Primary School**

# Fun

Fun is like a bouncy ball,
Bouncing round a room,
Yellow, bright and sunny,
Gets rid of any gloom.

Happy faces all around,
Rolling on the grassy ground,
Sweeties and vanilla ice cream,
I'm happy when I dream.

Birthday cake, my friends,
With them the fun doesn't end,
Fishing by the weeping willow,
Laying gently on my pillow.

Apple pie and friendly faces,
Families are going places,
Woolly hats and strawberry jam,
Sausages sizzling in a pan.

Pancakes flipping up and down,
Labradors that are chocolate-brown,
Teddy bears and cuddly toys,
Jelly beans for girls and boys.

Magicians and funny clowns,
Hot summer days and fluffy clouds,
Cuddling your dad and mum,
All of these are really fun.

**Amy Golesworthy (11)**
**Old Bexley CE Primary School**

# Black Tears

Sadness is like a dark funeral.
Sadness smells like burning paper that can never come back again.
Sadness tastes like a tasteless liquid that trickles
                                    down your throat forever.
Sadness looks like a pool of tears that never go away.
Sadness sounds like a repetitive bang that disappears when you cry.
Sadness feels like someone's died and left me in the world alone
                            with no one I know, I am still on my own!
Sadness reminds me of a shadow that never vanishes
                                and now I am followed *forever.*

**Shannice Richards-Hargreaves (10)**
Old Bexley CE Primary School

# Fear

Fear is black
I am going to be attacked.
Fear sounds like . . .
A dead rat and an evil bat
Fear tastes like . . .
Spiders with some evil riders.
Fear smells like . . .
A poisoned apple and pineapple
Fear looks like . . .
Glass and my mum's favourite vase.
Fear feels like . . .
Blood and some rotten gunge.

**Emmanuel Akinrinoye (9)**
**Parkway Primary School**

# Fun

When you're having fun
It's mostly in the sun
Where you would like to run.
Fun is green
It wouldn't make you mean.
Fun sounds like laughter.
Fun looks like happiness.
Fun is after disappointment.

**Ifeloju Ladele (9)**
**Parkway Primary School**

# The Tree

The tree reached out,
'Without a doubt
I will catch you
Whenever I want
When you hide behind me.
When you've gone home for a rest
I'll give you all my best
That I won't be there
For every moment
I don't care.
So when you come out tomorrow
I surely will borrow you,
So next time don't bother me
And I won't bother you anymore.
So think next time
I will be there waiting
For *yo-o-ou ha ha ha!*'

**Dembie Bowden (10)**
**Parkway Primary School**

# The Stars

Twirling stars in the sky,
How do they do it? I don't know how.
North, west, south or east, stars are everywhere.

Shooting stars are the best
Because they may grant your wishes,
And stars also can make pictures in the sky,
Rushing stars racing across the sky.
Shining stars are most interesting though.

**Sophie Duong  (10)**
**Parkway Primary School**

# Love

Love is pink,
It sounds like music,
Love tastes like a lolly you can lick,
It smells like roses,
Love looks like cheeks blushing,
Love feels like hearts rushing,
Love reminds me of God.

**Moyosore Adegbola  (8)**
**Parkway Primary School**

# Full Of Sadness

Sadness is pain, sadness is hurt,
Sadness is tears dropping down to your shirt.
Sadness feels like you're being left out.
It sounds like someone is gonna shout.
Sadness makes you cry,
Sometimes it wants to make you die.
Sadness, sadness, sadness,
Your life is full of sadness.

**Sally Nguyen (8)**
**Parkway Primary School**

# Planet Earth

Planet Earth drinks a lot of salty water,
Planet Earth eats a lot of layered land.
Best of all though
Planet Earth has a lot of funky friends.

Planet Earth is only just a heavy-weighted head,
Which contains a lot of tremendous things.
Its siblings are the other planets
And its parents are the slinky sun and muscular moon.

The sad thing is global warming,
It's supposed to have a cold forehead and neck.
Unfortunately, because of its friends
It is sadly having a hot temperature.

The cousins are the shiny stars
That glisten in space.
That we can see from Earth,
The ones that have extraordinary names.

**Winnie Lam  (11)**
**Parkway Primary School**

# Love

Love is like God's angel soaring,
Making a friend or maybe just scoring.
Someone out there is looking for you,
All you have to do is find them too.

My name's Bob and this is my job,
Telling this story to you.
Do you know, love comes from the Lord above.
He shares His love with all of us.

**Shaneece Bryan  (8)**
**Parkway Primary School**

# Darkness

Darkness was once a faraway shadow
Then you left me . . .
The feeling then came closer than ever
And happiness was now a faraway distant memory.

Darkness did not wait
It immediately took the bait
Hate started to form
A storm of unhappiness blew away all joy.

You've come back!
Then I see her.
I still wonder
Did you ever love me?

**Sophia Hou  (9)**
**Parkway Primary School**

# Anger And Love

Anger is like a fire in your heart.
Anger is a bad feeling.
Just think about love.
Love is free like a dove flying in the sky.
Love is like a loving couple joining together.
So, when you are angry, just think about love.

**Remalia Mills  (8)**
**Parkway Primary School**

# Penguins

These funny birds in fancy clothes
Have a white chest you see.
They've got blubber to keep them warm
Instead of a cup of tea.
These captivating creatures
Looking for their lunch
Along comes a fish
*Nibble . . . nibble . . . crunch!*

These efficient swimmers
Are graceful in the water
Gliding, swooping beautifully
But on land they dramatically alter.
These fascinating beings are called penguins
You never see them fly
Unlike other birds
High up in the sky.

**Charlotte Butler (11)**
**Perry Hall Primary School**

# My Day

At 7am, I wake up from a dream,
I'm rubbing my eyes,
Thinking 'bout whippy cream.

At 9am, I'm late for school,
My brother's still angry,
I made him late too.

At 10am, I've not done my homework,
I get a detention,
I hate Mrs Clerk.

At 12pm, I'm in the naughty room,
I'm writing out lines,
'I must bring in my . . .' *boom!*

At 12.30pm, the science room's blown,
The school is on fire!
'My things!' I moan.

As I run out of school,
I think to myself,
*No more school! Hooray!*

**Ai-Nhi Truong (11)**
**Perry Hall Primary School**

# My Invisible Pet

Spotty, stripes,
Frilly tights
Pink and spotty underwear,
That's my pet, I swear!

Scaly toes,
Feathers bright,
Nose with pointy warts on the end,
That's him, he's my friend!

Tentacles,
Stinging ends,
Bites you if you're not that nice,
Careful, he's got lice!

Froggy eyes,
Sticky tongue,
Goblins' pointy, hairy ears,
Healings in his tears!

Dustbin wheels,
Scabby legs,
Fingers with a pointy hook,
How does your pet look?

**Sophie McDonnell (11)**
**Perry Hall Primary School**

# The Mystery

A sound came from behind the tree,
*Rustle, rustle, rustle.*
My ears were glued to the mystery sound,
As people began to hustle,
As to what I had found.

It became louder, louder, closer, closer,
I'm not sure why.
When everything was quiet and still,
The mystery stopped,
And I gave a sigh.

I then saw the mystery,
That I could hear and see.
The shiny red, pink and blue
And silky, slimy scales.
He glared at me with eyes of flame!

His head and feet like a dragon,
His long fat tusks like a hog.
This big, mean monster I've not described,
Shall live in me for evermore!

**Annabelle Hall  (10)**
**Perry Hall Primary School**

# He's Mine

He's tall and hairy
And really quite scary
With blue and pink
Mixed together I think
He's mine, he's mine, he's mine

He's always wet
Like a fish, he's a pet
Yellow and green
It's his swimsuit, it gleams
He's mine, he's mine, he's mine

He's got big blue eyes
As big as four pies
His ears are round
They each weigh a pound
He's mine, he's mine, he's mine

He's kind with a heart of gold
And keeps every secret I've ever told
He's my best friend
Right until the end
And, he's mine, he's mine, he's mine.

**Dina Asher-Smith (11)**
**Perry Hall Primary School**

# The Sun

In the morning it lights up the sky
It's a wonderful sight
There is a rainbow of colours
Pink, orange, blue and white.

At lunch it is bright
The sky is blue and white
The sun gives off immense light
Very different to night.

At night the sun goes to bed
The moon comes up when you go to bed
As you sleep morning comes again
The cycle starts again.

**Torsten Deal  (10)**
**West Kent Health Needs Education Service**

# My Dog

He likes food.
He loves to play.
He is called Tyler.
He needs a walk every day.

He loves to scare.
He loves to run.
He likes to have fun.
He likes to share.

He loves a drink of tea.
He snuggles up with me.
He loves a biscuit too
But especially he loves me.

**Ben Presland  (10)**
**West Kent Health Needs Education Service**

# Cars

I love the noise of cars revving up
Big ones, small ones
Four-wheel drive
Red ones, blue ones, yellow ones too
Oh how I love cars -
Do you?

The ones that I love
Are Land Rovers
The model that I like is
Defender 110
Especially in black
With seats at the back.

**Matt McAuley (11)**
**West Kent Health Needs Education Service**

# Young Writers Information

We hope you have enjoyed reading this book - and that you will continue to enjoy it in the coming years.

If you like reading and writing poetry drop us a line, or give us a call, and we'll send you a free information pack.

Alternatively if you would like to order further copies of this book or any of our other titles, then please give us a call or log onto our website at www.youngwriters.co.uk

**Young Writers Information
Remus House
Coltsfoot Drive
Peterborough
PE2 9JX**

**(01733) 890066**